D1367093

LAND OF LIBERTY

AMERICA'S LANDSCAPE

LYNN M. STONE

Rourke
Publishing LLC
Vero Beach, Florida 32964

www.rourkepublishing.com

PHOTO CREDITS: All photos © Lynn M. Stone

Cover Photo: *Grand Canyon National Park, in the southwest United States, preserves the rugged beauty of the American landscape.*

Editor: Frank Sloan

Cover and page design by Nicola Stratford

Library of Congress Cataloging-in-Publication Data

Stone, Lynn M.
  America's landscape / Lynn M. Stone.
      p. cm. — (Land of liberty)
Summary: Describes the varied geography of the different parts of the United States.
Includes bibliographical references and index.
  ISBN 1-58952-310-5 (hardcover)
 1. United States—Geography—Juvenile literature. 2. Landscape—United States—Juvenile literature. [1. United States—Geography.] I. Title.

  E161.3 S76 2002
  917.3—dc21

                                                    2002004154

Printed in the USA

MP/W

Table of Contents

The snow-capped peaks of the Rockies in Wyoming are a highlight of the landscape of the West.

The American Landscape

America is a land of great size and variety. The **continental** United States reaches across the middle of North America from the Pacific Ocean to the Atlantic. Beyond the 48 continental states lie Alaska and Hawaii. They add even greater size and variety to the nation's landscape.

When Katharine Lee Bates wrote about the nation's beauty in "America the Beautiful," she got it right.

The Fourth Largest Country

America occupies more than 3 and one-half million square miles (more than 9 million square kilometers). It is the fourth largest country in the world, after Russia, Canada, and China.

Settlers had to cross the heights of the Continental Divide as they moved westward across America.

Katharine Lee Bates

Katharine Lee Bates once stood high on Pikes Peak in Colorado and viewed with amazement the **landscape** below. But Ms. Bates could have stood almost anywhere "from sea to shining sea" and been impressed by the view.

The view from Colorado's Rocky Mountain peaks is breathtaking.

Postcards

The natural American landscape unfolds like a giant book of postcards. There's a glacier on one card, a tropical beach on the next. The variety is endless.

Glacier National Park in Montana preserves postcard views of America's mountain landscape.

The Appalachians

Let's recall a few of the most scenic features of the American landscape. We'll start with real eye-catchers: mountains! The major mountain chain in the American east is the Appalachian range. It snakes from Maine southward into northern Alabama.

The Appalachian Mountains, shown here in Georgia, stretch northward into Maine.

The Rockies

In the west, the mighty Rockies form the backbone of the North American continent. They reach from Alaska southward through Canada and into Idaho, Montana, Wyoming, Colorado, and New Mexico. Many peaks in the Rockies stand more than 14,000 feet (4,270 meters) tall.

The mighty Rockies are in the American west.

The Pacific Coast

A rugged chain of coastal mountains stretches along the Pacific coast of Washington, Oregon, and California. Two mountain peaks in this region, Mount St. Helens and Lassen, are active volcanoes!

Where land meets sea: The Pacific Ocean borders the west coast of America from Alaska to California.

American bison graze on the prairie grasses of the Western plains.

"Amber Waves of Grain"

There is far more to the American landscape than mountains, of course. The "fruited plains" of "America the Beautiful" lie largely between the Appalachians and the Rockies. They make up much of middle and western America. The old, natural plains landscape is covered with forests and **prairies**. But much of the plains country is cropland with "amber waves of grain," as Ms. Bates wrote.

America's Forests

Most of America's mountains are covered with dense forests. The north woods of Maine, New York, Michigan, Wisconsin, and Minnesota are largely evergreen forests of spruce and pine.

Autumn leaves blaze below the snowy Green Mountain forests of Vermont.

Marshes of the Everglades are dotted with islands of semitropical trees.

Evergreens give way to colorful **broadleaf** forests farther south. And in southern Florida, the nation has a true subtropical forest.

Other Landforms

The forests of the East thin out in the Midwest. They give way to sweeping meadows of grass and sagebrush. In the dry Southwest, the landscape changes to desert—cactus country.

Great marshes, like the Everglades, and inland lakes are other scenic parts of the American landscape. The largest of American lakes, the Great Lakes, lie in the nation's upper Midwest.

The warm, dry Sonoran Desert stretches across much of southern Arizona.

Hawaii has volcano lands and the wettest rain forest on earth. Northern Alaska has endless miles of Arctic **tundra**. Mmm. "America the Beautiful" missed a few things, it seems.

The Alaskan tundra is warm with autumn color even in September drizzle.

Glossary

alpine (AL pyne) — of high mountain areas, such as alpine meadows

broadleaf (BRAWD leef) — referring to trees with wide leaves that change color each autumn and fall, such as maple leaves

continental (CAHN tuh nen tul) — referring to the 48 connected United States on the North American mainland

landforms (LAND formz) — features of the Earth's surface

landscape (LAND skape) — a wide view of natural scenery, especially inland

prairie (PRAYR ee) — a natural grassland

tundra (TUN druh) — the carpet of tiny plants and shrubs that covers much of the land of the far north

Index

Further Reading

Fowler, Allan. *Living in the Mountains.* Children's Press, 2000
Vieira, Linda. *Ever-Living Tree: The Life and Times of a Coast Redwood.* Walker and Company, 1996
Younger, Barbara. *Purple Mountain Majesties: The Story of Katharine Lee Bates and America the Beautiful.* Penguin Putnam, 1998

Websites to Visit

National Parks at http://www.us-national-parks.net/
National Park Service at http://www.nps.gov/parks.html

About the Author

Lynn Stone is the author of more than 400 children's nonfiction books. He is a talented natural history photographer as well. Lynn, a former teacher, travels worldwide to photograph wildlife in its natural habitat.